The Tree

Illustrated by Christian Broutin
Created by Pascale de Bourgoing
and Gallimard Jeunesse

MOONLIGHT PUBLISHING/FIRST DISCOVERY

KU-197-752

A shiny brown conker!

What is there hiding inside
this spiky green husk?

A conker
is a kind of chestnut.
A chestnut is the seed
of a chestnut tree.
Slowly it grows and
a tiny tree
shoots up.

Roots reach down
into the ground under the tree,
finding food and water.

At the end of winter, buds
sit at the end of
every branch and twig,
waiting for the sun to warm
them and stir them into life.

Slowly the
flowers grow
into chestnuts.

It's summer.
The chestnuts
ripen inside
their shells.

At the beginning
of autumn,
the ripe chestnuts
fall to the ground,
ready to take root
and grow into new trees.

Look at the
leaves changing
colour before
they fall.

The winter
trees are
bare.

Trees are very big plants.
Their branches, their bark, their roots
give food and shelter to all sorts
of different animals.

Look! Can you tell
which tree
is which
by their different
shapes and colours?

Beech trees can be very tall.

Maple trees turn a
brilliant orange in autumn.

Poplars grow tall
and pointed.

Weeping willows
have drooping branches.

The birch is
light and slender.

All trees have different leaves and fruit. Learn how to recognise them.

Sweet chestnuts have long thin leaves with little teeth along the edge.

Hazel trees have heart-shaped leaves.

Oak leaves have rounded edges.

Sweet chestnut

Hazel nuts

Acorn

Walnut leaves
look like a line of
smaller leaves together.

Maple leaves
have five points.

Walnut

Maple seeds
have wings.

Some trees
keep their leaves
all year round.
They are called
evergreens.

Cypress

Sequoia

Fir tree

Their fruit are hard wooden cones, with the seeds inside.

Their leaves are
thin and spiky.
They do not change
colour in autumn.

Umbrella pine

Cedar

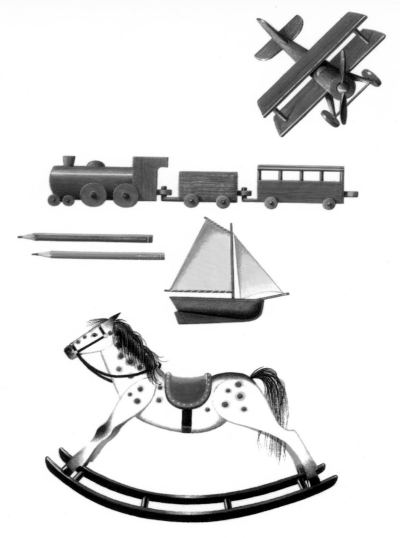

You can make a lot of different things with
the wood that comes from trees.

Wood shavings,
crushed and squeezed together,
make wood pulp.
Wood pulp makes paper.
With that paper,
you can make a book ...
about trees!

<u>Now discover the exciting secrets of:</u>

Cats
The Ladybird
The Egg
Fruit
Vegetables
Weather

All titles available in the same series

Translator: Sarah Matthews
Editorial adviser: Dr Jane Mainwaring

ISBN 1 85103 087 5
©1989 by Editions Gallimard
English text © 1990 by Moonlight Publishing Ltd
First published in the United Kingdom 1990
by Moonlight Publishing Ltd, 36 Stratford Road, London W8

Printed in Italy